Thoughts in Rhyme From a Contentious Time

Original Poems & Parodies
Written During the Trump Years
2015-2021

Linda Sadick Furman

Thoughts in Rhyme From a Contentious Time —1st ed.

Paperback: 978-1-7378549-0-6
Hardcover: 978-1-7378549-1-3

Dedication

To my father, Kenneth Sadick,
the "Leader of the Band"
in so many ways –
especially with poetry.

To my mother, Norma Davidson Sadick,
who gave me the gifts of love, patience, and music.

Thank You!

Written on the 4th of July, 2004

How often I've told you,
My dear Mom and Dad,
That you're both loved and greatly admired.
You've been wonderful folks
Through the good times and bad –
Finer parents could not be desired!

Have I ever expressed, though,
The pride in my heart
When upon the war years I reflect?
The sacrifices that
Kept you apart for so long –
How you've earned my respect!

From the letters Mom wrote
To the missions Dad flew,
Through the war's seeming endless duration,
What Tom Brokaw declares
In his book is so true:
Yours is the Greatest Generation.

So, thank you, not only
For love and for trust
And instilling strong values in me;
But also for braving
The dangers you must
Have faced so your kids could be free!

Ken Sadick with his P-47 Thunderbolt, c. 1944

Contents

Preface

I grew up in a home full of love, music and poetry. My dad wrote poems for every occasion and my mother played the piano. We all sang – in the car and at home. My older sister was also a poet, but my poetry gene didn't kick in until I was about 40. I began by writing songs to teach math skills to my 4th graders – everything from long division to how to add unlike fractions. Soon I was writing song parodies and poems for anything and everything I felt strongly about!

The Trump years gave rise to a huge number of political song parodies, "the likes of which have never been seen before," as Trump himself would say. I have so enjoyed the work of like-minded, talented fellow parody-writers and performers on YouTube, such as the incomparable Randy Rainbow, Roy Zimmerman, Founders Sing, SongBird, and others.

From the beginning of his candidacy to the waning days of his presidency, Trump's recent time in the political spotlight has been the most stressful fifty, er, five years of many of our lives. Some of us wrote letters to the editor and staged protests. Some had heated arguments with family members and friends. I chose to volunteer for the 2018 and 2020 Democratic campaigns and to write poetry and song parodies. What you are about to read was my therapy. I hope you enjoy it!

Note: The poems and comments in this book reflect my own opinions. The behavior and incidents they are based upon, however, are factual.

Introduction

I want to share a poem that I wrote in 1997, while teaching middle school. It explains my outlook on bullying, which has everything to do with my Trump-era poetry. We teachers had just attended a seminar on the subject, and the keynote speaker made these two points that reverberated in my mind afterward:

1) Students should spend at least as much time looking inward as they do on their looks.
2) The bully's behavior reveals much more about the bully than it does about the victim.

After only a few days, the following poem popped out. While it was written for 6th, 7th, and 8th graders, it applies to people of all ages. How I wish Donald Trump had absorbed this lesson during his formative years!

Don't Forget Your Character!

3/23/1997

When you look in the mirror do you check out your face?
Do you hope your hair's not gone berserk?
If your clothes look ok, do you exit the place?
You might look great, but still be a jerk.

Take time to inspect what you look like inside.
Would you want you, yourself for a friend?
Do your words and your actions fill you with pride?
Do you mean what you say – or pretend?

The kids who neglect to check inside each day
Do not care if their teasing turns mean.
"Who cares? It was only a joke!" they would say.
The wounds caused are real, but unseen.

The way you treat others tells more about you
Than it does about those you may hurt.
With put-downs you're on top a minute or two,
But it's you who is down in the dirt.

With a word or a look you reveal who you are,
So take care every day when you've dressed.
Check to see that your character is up-to-par.
It's the part of you that is the best!

CHAPTER 1

2015-2016 - There's No Way He's Gonna Win...

When Donald Trump announced his candidacy in June 2015, strong opinions immediately began to form. His years as a bon vivant and playboy, "successful" New York business-man, casino owner, and reality TV celebrity had made his arrogance widely known. His speech that day, characterizing Mexicans as rapists who bring drugs and crime to the US, intensified the country's polarization, separating Americans into Trump supporters and opponents.

I wrote my first political poem after a particularly negative series of speeches given by then-candidate Trump. I updated it three times: after Trump won the primary, after he became president and after the pandemic hit in early 2020. This poem has a distinct pattern, with three rhyming words required in the second part of each verse. It was fun to write!

PRESIDENT Trump? Oh no...!

August 2015

Much to our surprise, we've begun to realize
Trump could be our next president.
If he gets elected we'll need to be protected
From all his mean sentiment.

He claims he's successful, without time to be respectful
Says whatever - and expects we'll agree.
If I ran the forum we all would just ignore him
And find another nominee!

Disagreeing will result in Trump being insultin'–
Bad example for our kids to see.
He may be good at dealing but I have a nagging feeling
He's lacking diplomacy.

Trump may be speaking what a lot of folks are thinking
But his attitude is stinking, I fear.
Don't want our kids to emulate him. Hoping someone will deflate him
Before the election year!

September 2016

We survived primary season, but I can't discern the reason
Voters made Trump their nominee.
Out of 17 contenders any other would be better –
The pride of the GOP.

Now the party has no voice - they are saddled with their choice –
This condescending, rude, and boisterous dolt.
Our only hope for his rejection is the general election,
So, people, ya gotta vote!!

June 2018

Well, November came and went – Our 45th president
Is none other than Donald Trump.
His behavior is pathetic. He's not kind or empathetic.
To most everyone he's a grump.
Our alliances he muddies, treats our enemies like buddies,
Hates the media but studies TV.

Thinks border safety we attain by locking kids in links of chain
As their parents flee tyranny.

The economy was moving and the job outlook improving,
But Trump started a trading war.
It's impossible to share if Trump keeps imposing tariffs
To even the trading score.

All the goods will be expensive and the rhetoric offensive,
But the president's defensive and tough.
We will soon be isolated, all our friendships decimated.
Of his "winning" we've had enough!

April, 2020

2020 finally came and we hope it ends his reign.
Trump thinks his power is absolute.
His supporters still believe him while the rest of us are grievin'
For the murder of honest truth.

He dismisses the pandemic while the learned academics
Warn the threat is still systemic, at best...
Won't be anybody resting as long as Trump's denying testing,
Ignoring the states' protests.

When this history is written, though no fault he is admittin',
Time reveals reality.
He made governors and mayors find supplies and ventilators,
Denying responsibility.

Sends his Trumpists to protest the shutdown 'cause they feel
oppressed
By guidelines experts who know best have advised.
We'll likely have a second wave if the people don't behave,
Our very lives will be compromised!

In 2013 I had the once-in-a-lifetime experience of riding a mule to the bottom of the Grand Canyon. I was terrified! But, encouraged and supported by my then-fiancé – now husband – Bill, on the mule behind me, it turned out to be one of the best things I have ever done. My mount was a steady and reliable one named Maude.

By the summer of 2016 I had decided that I would rather vote for Maude than for either of the two major candidates running for President. I composed a poem to that effect and set it to my own original tune, which I then sang, accompanied by my son, Brian on guitar and recorded by my daughter-in-law, Robyn - and posted it on YouTube. (Hear it by searching "Election 2016 Vote Mule!")

VOTE MULE in 2016!

6/10/2016

I've never been so aggravated
By any presidential contest.
How does a narcissist bully
Get people to think he's the best?

Trump's like a belligerent school boy.
His actions are never his fault.
Insults and slander he hurls with abandon -
Not even a judge could escape his assault!

CHORUS:

Oh, the Elephants put up a jackass,
And the Donkey I'm not sure I trust.
With a Mule as our third-party candidate
We'll get where we're going – or bust!

Miss Hillary's looking to lead us.
She's been living it since '92.
The mess with her emails will not go away –
Her detractors, she has quite a few.

What really went down in Benghazi?
Explain it – I'm waiting to hear.
I don't think I can cast my ballot
For either of these two this year.

CHORUS:

Oh, the Elephants put up a jackass,
And the Donkey I'm not sure I trust.
With a Mule as our third-party candidate
We'll get where we're going – or bust!

Now, mules would be good in a crisis,
Where others would panic, it's true.
You may think that they're being stubborn,
They're actually thinking things through.

I'm giving my vote to Miss Maude.
She's my mule from the Grand Canyon Trail.
You want toughness, endurance and brains in your leader?
She's got it where others have failed.

Maude's loyal, sure-footed and patient.
What more does a candidate need?
She's decent and totally honest.
No words that insult – and no emails to read!

So, get on the mule bandwagon
And turn this election around.
Write in Maude, the most ethical candidate.
Let's change red states and blue states to brown!

Oh, the Elephants put up a jackass,
And the Donkey I'm not sure I trust.
With a Mule as our third-party candidate
We'll make a strong showing,
Her poll numbers growing,
We'll get where we're going – or bust!

CHAPTER 2

2017-2018 – Get In, Sit Down, and Hold On!

After his inauguration, Trump continued the name-calling, belittling, and condemnation of the press that would mar his entire presidency and overshadow his every accomplishment. Trump's toxic behavior resulted in a loss of respect for him, both at home and around the world. Rather than soften his attitude, he intensified his attacks on anyone who opposed him.

In early 2017, while accepting a lifetime achievement award at the Golden Globes, Meryl Streep called out the newly elected president for bullying and disrespectful behavior. Trump responded in his usual knee-jerk fashion by calling Meryl "overrated." I felt left out! Here's my whimsical poem on that serious subject.

Call Me Overrated Too!

1/13/2017, Revised 6/4/2020

I want to be called overrated by Trump.
It's my new goal in life, don't you see?
But you have to be famous, no ordinary chump —
You must be a celebrity.

Now, I am not Meryl or Seinfeld or Megyn
Or the "Hamilton" actors so able,
Not a past president like Obama or Clinton —
They received the overrated label.

I'm not part of the press, like Krauthammer or Will,
Nor Jon Stewart, who was on TV.
General Mattis and McCain up on Capitol Hill
Were dishonored — so why not me?

Why won't he insult ME? I'm feeling neglected
And want to be part of that crew
Of intelligent people who are well-respected
For stating their own points of view.

Trump thinks only those who support him are cool.
There's no room in his mind for the rest.
Why can't he see name-calling makes him the fool
And leaves most of us unimpressed?

He's made a career of attacking detractors
But it's he who's committed the gaffe.
From now on, the pundits, politicians, and actors
Should just simply point and laugh!

In mid-2017, Trump was rude to America's allies at the NATO summit. It was shocking and embarrassing. Former teaching colleagues confessed that some of their students were emulating the president's negative behavior. This poem was written in response to that distressing news.

A Cautionary Tale

About Karma

6/1/2017

To our dear sons and daughters, please listen
To this lesson we hope you will learn.
Whatever you say and whatever you do –
What to others you give will return.

Take a look at the man in the White House
And you'll realize karma can bite.
Put-downs and blame fill his daily harangues,
Yet he still thinks respect is his right.

Did Trump's mom teach her son about kindness?
Did his dad ever mention respect?
Only as it relates to what's given to HIM,
Not the other way 'round, I suspect.

He's been rude to the leaders we cherish –
Those from Germany, England, and more.
If anyone dares criticize what he says
He tweets insults to even the score.

At his first NATO summit in May of this year
Trump pushed Montenegro's leader aside,
Got in front, never looked at him, straightened his coat,
Stuck his chin out in arrogant pride.

Kids get that cutting in front is unfair,
So why doesn't our own president?
If a teacher observed such behavior, you know
To the back of the line he'd be sent!

Trump needs to look in the mirror
When searching for someone to blame.
His own words and his actions are bringing him down,
Not the media, as he would claim.

He thinks he's been treated unfairly,
Too self-centered to ever observe
That sooner or later the universe gives you
The karma that you deserve.

Seeing the media constantly fall for Trump's deliberate attention-seeking ploys, with his daily rude and outlandish tweets, frustrated me to no end. It just made him act out more! Why couldn't they ignore some of it? After all, the technique works on children. This limerick aims to get that point across.

Advice for the Media

7/5/2017

If the media's really astute
And reporting-the-facts resolute,
Then each rude, hateful tweet
Needs to take a back seat
So its power will finally dilute.

Yet, the media's duped by this ruse,
As Trump verbally tightens the screws.
The press, thrown off track,
Keeps ignoring the fact
No one's focused on critical news.

So, don't fall for his tricks, like before.
When Trump tweets, use restraint and ignore.
No attention or care
Is Trump's biggest nightmare.
Hope he won't want to play anymore.

In August 2018, when Trump uttered the words, "Fake, fake disgusting news!" I was enraged – so I grabbed a pad and pencil and composed this poem in about 20 minutes.

The Real Enemy of the People

8/2/2018

"Fake, fake, disgusting news!"
Anything that doesn't share Trump's views.
Never, since the Pilgrims landed
Have leaders ridiculed and branded
Journalists who disagree
As traitors and our enemy.
The First Amendment will soon apply
To just one outlet. We decry
The muffling of the Fourth Estate
As Trump attempts to make us "great."

Do we live in a fascist state?
Does Trump really desire to create
A country without speech that's free?
Without the right to disagree?
He took an oath – swore to uphold
The Constitution, but he boldly
Mocks it with his lies and hate,
Yet, congress will not set him straight.

Lie upon lie he tells with ease,
Believed by all his devotees.
He's president of just his base.
The rest feel we have been erased.
Supporters, now an angry mob
At rallies – They'll complete his job.
If soon a journalist is dead,
It surely will be on Trump's head.

CHAPTER 3

2019 - Beatings Will Continue Until Morale Improves

In 2019, Donald Trump began his re-election campaign efforts in earnest. His strategy seemed to include ratcheting up the hate and blame by demonizing anyone who was not a loyal Trump supporter. If that meant dividing the country, so be it. It was all about winning.

Trump especially hated the late, Republican Arizona Senator John McCain. He was a decorated Navy pilot during the Vietnam War, who was captured and tortured for five years. Trump hated that John was so revered for his service and sacrifice. When asked if he thought McCain was a war hero, he declared, "He was a war hero because he was captured. I like people who weren't captured, ok?" He also hated that John was willing to reach across the congressional aisle to work for the good of the country. McCain earned Trump's ultimate rage by giving a thumbs-down vote to the repeal of Obamacare.

I wrote a parody about Trump's obsession with McCain to the tune of "That's Why the Lady is a Tramp," a 1937 Rodgers & Hart song, written for the musical, *Babes in Arms*.

That's Why The Donald Hates McCain

3/21/2019

VERSE 1:

There once were two men, both political guys.
One spoke his truth and the other denies,
Spewing his hate with continuous lies.
Why does The Donald hate McCain?

VERSE 2:

One fooled the service, claimed his foot bone was spurred.
One went to Vietnam and torture endured.
Trump can't compete with John's honors conferred.
That's why the Trumpster hates McCain.

CHORUS:

There are some facts that Trump won't reveal –
Docs from Chris Steele
Came to light
Post-election night!
He doesn't care, he would rather complain,
Since he can't equal John McCain.

VERSE 3:

For voting no, John endured his assault.
Blamed only him, said it was all his fault.
Other Republicans, too, caused it to halt,
But Trump would rather hate McCain.

Trump won't relent – he is riddled with hate.
He is so jealous of a man who was great.
Trump won't admit he can't obliterate
The life of service that's McCain.

CHORUS:

There is no kindness we can discern.
When will he learn?
He'd be wise
To apologize.
There is no way Trump will ever attain
The same respect as John McCain!

With Trump's hate and vitriol out of control, many wondered why GOP leaders throughout the country stood by and said nothing. They knew they would be belittled, demonized, and primaried in their next elections if they dared challenge Trump, so they kept quiet. Nobody would speak up. I know – I asked!

An Open Letter to the GOP and Congressional Republicans Who Support Trump

5/29/2019

When did it no longer matter
If our president's an honorable man?
When did you trade in your values?
And I wonder just how can you stand

That he butters-up Kim Jong-un
And denies Russians plotted to hack
Our elections, our freedom, our own way of life?
You stay silent while we head off track.

When did it start to be normal
To hear name-calling, insults and lies
Coming out of the White House we once revered,
From a man most Americans despise?

The economy's good – so the rest doesn't count?
Is money what you value most?
How can you honestly measure success
Built on ambition so grandiose?

I do NOT want to hear and WILL NOT accept,
"Well, what about that one or this?"
NO previous candidate or president
Matches Trump's lies and viciousness.

He'll lie to your face, even if there is proof
To the contrary – yet you believe.
He's cheated and conned and played you for fools.
You can't possibly be that naïve!

Will you ever decide that enough is enough?
Is there not a red line he has crossed?
How bad does his behavior have to become
Before your loyalty to him is lost?

Wake up! We are losing the allies we trust,
As our enemies advance for the kill.
Trump's inviting them in, while he slams the door
On our friends, who now lack our good will.

When in the rear mirror historians assess
The reign of this tyrant at hand,
Those who stood by while democracy died
Will be blamed for not taking a stand.

The silence from the Republicans began to really get to me. Trump grew even bolder. His verbal abuse grew more hateful, racist, and bigoted. The mood of much of the country resembled that of people living with an abusive family member. It was becoming intolerable, but still, nobody who Trump might have listened to was willing to speak out.

The Silence is Deafening

7/16/2019

The words Trump has said
Are the bigoted kind.
What is sadder instead
Is the silence we find
From the party that's red.
Are they of the same mind?

Or is not speaking out
Against racist speech
More likely about
An attempt to reach
The voters who no doubt
Agree with the breach?

We'll look back one day
On his tyrant-like reign,
And history will say
Those who dared to complain
Loved the USA
More than those who refrain.

Labor to keep alive

in your breast that

little spark of celestial fire,

called conscience.

George Washington

It got so bad that, at his rallies, Trump began referring to immigrants and others he didn't want to be in this country as an "infestation," a word used to great effect by Adolf Hitler. He described the Jews as an "infestation" in his hate-filled speeches during WWII. Was this still the United States of America, a representative democracy, or were we becoming a dictatorship? Words really do matter. For this poem, I rhymed, or nearly rhymed, every other line with "infested" to make my point.

Infestation of Hate

8/1/2019

Trump declares we are being infested
By immigrants, rodents and rats,
And Democrats, who he's detested
Since the first China-made MAGA hats.

He riled up his base and suggested
That congressmen who disagree
Return to their "places," congested
With vermin – he states this with glee.

His supporters have loudly protested
That Trump's only speaking what's true.
But racist tropes he has invested
Are aimed at a specific few.

Never mind they've been duly elected
To serve in the congress he hates.
Never mind that free speech is protected.
There's no room in his world for debates.

If Trump's policies they have contested,
Then they must hate our country, as well.
Of this notion we must be divested.
This idea we have to dispel!

Love of country is hardly reflected
In loyalty to party or man.
When hate is too often protected
Then the people must do what they can.

We must become reinvested
In the values that we once held.
Our mettle has been sorely tested.
It is beyond time that we rebelled.

Yes, our country's becoming infested,
But it's not the kind Trump would avow.
It's hate and lies now manifested
That's the vermin we cannot allow.

In 2019, some of Trump's closest associates were under indictment for various crimes discovered in the Mueller report. Trump was feeling boxed in, still blaming the "fake news" and the Democrats for the investigation. By October the deal Trump tried to make in late July with the leader of Ukraine, trading arms for dirt on his opponent for the 2020 election, Joe Biden, came to light. This quid pro quo led to his impeachment in the House. This parody is to the tune of "Fame," the title song from the 1980 movie of the same name, written by Michael Gore and Dean Pitchford.

BLAME!

10/2/2019

VERSE:

When you look at me how can you disagree?
I have not done anything wrong.
Give me time to string you along with lies.

The guilt is not with me. No impropriety!
There has been no quid pro quo,
I just want dirt on Joe!

CHORUS:

Find somebody to blame! (BLAME!)
Nothing is my fault, no never.
Subpoena the records – just try.
I'll get my cronies together –
Tweets through my fingers will fly!

The deep state and Dems out to get me,
Ruin my good name they'll try.
The whistle-blower upset me,
Phone calls were declassified.

VERSE:

First Crooked Hillary, then Nancy Pelosi,
Adam Schiff – they all have no class.
So unfair, the way they're harassing me.

Don't care who gets bruised, lives ruined, who gets used.
I will always come out on top,
Lie and smear 'til they stop!

CHORUS:

Find somebody to blame! (BLAME!)
I'll be dictator forever.
My people will make it come true.
Rudy and Mike are too clever
To let this be my Waterloo.

Polls and the fake news still plague me.
Hope that my comrades don't cave.
What if Bill Barr cannot save me...
Is it too late to behave...?

Here's another impeachment parody, to the tune of "There is Nothing Like a Dame," from the 1949 musical, *South Pacific*, written by Rogers & Hammerstein.

There is Nothing I've Done Wrong

10/9/2019

VERSES: (2)

I have money, I have fame. I know all the greatest words.
I know all about trade deficits, the Turkish and the Kurds.
I know more about Islamic State than all the generals do.
What ain't I got ?
A G@!-#%mn clue!

I'm a genius who is stable, with a very massive brain.
My IQ is higher than the rest - for them I have disdain.
I have great and unmatched wisdom, more than everyone combined.
What have I lost?
My freakin' mind!

I don't understand why nobody gets me.
All this talk of impeachment just upsets me.

CHORUS:

There is nothing I've done wrong! Nothing in the world.
Investigate me all day long – You'll find I have done nothing wrong.

VERSE:

They say I'm king of Israel. I am the chosen one.
I alone can fix the country. I will never be out-done.
And if anyone defies me they will surely feel my wrath.
Some even call me
A psychopath!

The Democrats who say I lie and cheat and obstruct – they are the reason
I want to charge Adam Schiff & Nancy Pelosi with treason!

CHORUS: (3)

There is nothing in my past. I have been a saint.
All my supporters are steadfast – This impeachment I will outlast.

So I tell a lie or two. Everybody does.
I can change your point of view by repeating what is untrue.

Fox and Friends will have my back, just you wait and see!
They'll protect me from the flak as we plan our counterattack!

VERSE:

I'll obstruct and stall and stonewall – I will never testify.
I will call this kangaroo court what it is – unjustified.
There's no limit to the lengths I'll go to keep things under wraps,
From documentation to my income tax!

CHORUS:

There's so many I can blame – men I used to trust.
Now they're patsies I can frame and throw under the moving bus!

There are no crooks in my clan.
Nobody looks like me – tan.
Nobody lies like I can.
I'm a despised businessman.
An old and tired ladies' man,
But I'm admired by the Klan!
I'm the best our country ever has had
If you are judging the ones who've been bad.
Unscrupulous, illiterate, belligerent, immoral madman!

CHAPTER 4

2020-21 – Voting, a Virus, and Vicious Lies

The year 2020 will go down in the history books right alongside Watergate, the pandemic of 1918, and the racial unrest of the 1960's – only we had reprises of all three!

Unlike Nixon, Trump didn't resign when the House brought articles of impeachment against him, since he knew he had the backing of the Republican-led Senate. Sure enough, its members refused to call any witnesses and went straight to a vote to acquit him.

At this point, Trump felt invincible. Unfortunately, there was this little germ – a new virus, COVID-19, about to destroy everything in its path. How did Trump respond? He lied, insisting that it was nothing, and that it would magically disappear. He claimed he didn't want people to panic, but how could Americans make informed decisions without the facts? We later discovered that he had admitted on tape in an interview with investigative journalist, Bob Woodward, that he knew as early as February that this was a highly contagious virus, which was many times more deadly than the most "strenuous flus."

By March, the virus was declared a world-wide pandemic. Trump accused the Democrats of purposely exaggerating the severity of the virus in order to ruin his re-election chances. He made governors source and purchase their own PPE for hospitals, forcing them to compete for scarce supplies. Governors who were his allies or were nice to him received more funding and equipment. Thousands of people were infected and died, while Trump continued to minimize the situation. Soon the United States led the entire world in per capita COVID cases and deaths.

As soon as the numbers began to subside in late spring – and against the advice of epidemiologists and scientists – Trump urged those governors who had locked down their states to re-open them. Armed Trump supporters stormed some state capitol buildings, demanding the same. While a right-wing group's plot to kidnap and kill Michigan's governor, Gretchen Whitmer, was thwarted by law enforcement, Trump continued to discredit her at his rallies.

In May, the death of an unarmed Black man, George Floyd, added to the national tragedy and sparked massive protests across the country. Trump strong-armed the protestors instead of listening to their grievances, making things infinitely worse.

After spiking in July, a more severe COVID wave hit in October, and cases reached an all-time high. Despite this, Trump and many of his supporters refused to wear masks and mocked those who did. Daily new case counts that surpassed 100,000 became the norm by election day and, having been completely politicized, COVID was on the minds of voters. Trump continued to ignore the experts and to publicly minimize the virus. The number of jobs, businesses, and lives lost was utterly devastating.

In April 2020, during a news conference with his COVID task force, Trump pushed an unproven Malaria drug with serious heart-related side-effects, hydroxychloroquine, as a cure for COVID-19. He also suggested that the task force look into the use of lights, or the ingestion of bleach or other disinfectants as potential ways of killing the virus. A few people in the US actually followed his advice, drank bleach, and became very sick. Trump was ridiculed for his recommendations, but he insisted that he was just being sarcastic.

Can you say, "Gaslight?" Video of the news conference shows that he was completely serious.

The 1960 hit by Carole King and Gerry Goffin, "Will You Still Love Me Tomorrow," was the inspiration for this parody.

Will You Gaslight Us Tomorrow?

4/25/2020

Your daily briefings were informing,
Then FDA put out a warning.
You mention cures that science can't define.
Will you gaslight us tomorrow?

You told us try hydroxychloroquine.
"What have you got to lose, and you might win!"
Now, doctors say it shouldn't be prescribed.
Will you gaslight us tomorrow?

You said, with words fantastic,
"A shot of cleaner maybe helps."
Now you claim you were sarcastic.
No one else believes that but yourself!

Will you just keep on deceiving?
'Cause not one word we are believing.
Must we accept your ignorance and lies
When you gaslight us tomorrow?

Must we accept your ignorance and lies
When you gaslight us tomorrow?
When you gaslight us tomorrow?
When you gaslight us tomorrow?

On a walk in May, I had the Randy Rainbow parody, "Before He Tweets," in my head, where toward the end he sings, "Hey, USA, we just elected us a mean girl!" I had to write this poem on my phone so I wouldn't forget it!

The Mean Girl in the White House

5/20/2020

We elected a mean girl in 20-16.
Though he looks like a man, he is not.
He acts like the bullies that we have all seen,
And he lies every time he is caught.
He hasn't progressed much beyond 7th grade,
When name-calling makes you seem cool.
The lies and the put-downs that he has displayed
Only make him look childish and cruel.
Why some will excuse him I just can't explain.
They ignore his tirades and insults
And his penchant for finding others to blame,
Reminiscent of members of cults.
This pandemic exposed his ineptitude
At a time when a leader was needed.
His ill-tempered and arrogant attitude
In November must be defeated!

Just when it seemed that things couldn't possibly get worse, the world witnessed the murder of George Floyd in late May. He was killed by a white police officer who held his knee on George's neck for over nine horrific minutes. As the unarmed, handcuffed Black man lay face down, gasping for breath, two other officers aided in restraining him, and a third ensured that no bystanders intervened.

There were massive protests in every major city in America, calling for criminal justice reform. While the demonstrations continued, Trump chose to prove his domination of the streets and his devotion to God with a photo op at St. John's Church in Lafayette Square, across from the White House. The peaceful protesters were cleared out with tear gas just before he arrived.

In the style of Dudley Randall's poem, "The Ballad of Birmingham," describing the 1963 bombing of the 16th Street Baptist Church in that city, I wrote this poem to chronicle this awful, bizarre and un-Christian event. I also used a word that rhymes with "square" at the end of every other line.

The Clash in Lafayette Square

6/3/2020

In May 2020 our nation exploded
In anger and utter despair.
Justice for people of color eroded –
Lives lost that the police didn't spare.

Many took to the streets all over this land
To make our leaders aware
That deadly force no longer will stand,
Nor a system of justice unfair.

In desperate need of leadership,
We hoped Trump would declare
His empathy and bipartisanship,
But his focus was always elsewhere.

Instead, domination was on his mind,
As he called the troops to ensnare
Protesters, along with the looters they'd find.
Their message – he just didn't care.

He walked to St. John's with a Bible in hand,
Not kneeling or saying a prayer
While peaceful protesters were forced to disband
As tear-gas filled the air.

When history relates the uprising we've seen
Trump's character will be laid bare,
Revealing his desire to crush and demean
By the Clash in Lafayette Square.

After watching people of every ethnicity marching in solidarity for criminal justice reform, I decided to express my feelings to people of color with this poem.

You Are Not Alone

6/20/2020

I am a white woman. I thought I was "woke"
About race and acceptance and such.
But I never suspected a system so broken
Would cause me to get in touch
With the horrors that people of color still face.
I had never before realized
That the simple act of just going someplace
Can mean safety and lives jeopardized.

Will you be detained, not allowed to pass through?
Or be killed with impunity?
These fears never entered my own point of view
'Til George Floyd felt the officer's knee.
Now I see it, I get it, I understand why
Unjustly mistreated, you rise.
No longer alone, whites are joining the cry
For equality – We empathize.

We join in this cause. We can do it – we must,
For the sake of those living and passed,
Hold accountable those who violate our trust:
Equal protection for all at last.
Now, it's time to do more – Overhaul and assess,
New beliefs and behavior conform.
Enact laws that demand what we seek to redress –
Equal justice must become the norm.

Dr. Anthony Fauci, director of the National Institute of Allergy and Infectious Diseases since 1984, is one of the world's leading experts on infectious diseases. He has worked for every administration since Ronald Reagan's.

This year, he became the scapegoat for the pandemic in a dangerous campaign of misinformation. Dr. Fauci spoke honestly about the pandemic, daring to contradict the president's false optimism and lies about the virus. Trump, jealous of the attention being paid to Dr. Fauci, began to publicly discredit him. Conspiracy theories circulated on the internet, stating that Dr. Fauci was somehow involved in unleashing COVID-19 on the world. He and his family began to receive death threats – for telling us the truth!

I thought a song showing support for Dr. Fauci might be appreciated. "I Believe in You," from the 1961 musical, How to Succeed in Business Without Really Trying, music and lyrics by Frank Loesser, was the perfect choice for this parody.

We Believe in You!

7/14/2020

You have wisdom gained since you no longer are in your youth.
Yet you are often blamed for proclaiming your science and truth.
We believe in you!
We believe in you!

We need the voice of good, solid judgment in times such as these,
Amid the lies and stress, you address truth while Trump disagrees.
Oh, we believe in you!
We believe in you!

And when our faith in the government all but falls apart,
We've but to listen to your advice
Because you're smart –
Truly smart!

Please don't stop speaking out! You're the doc upon whom we rely.
You give us honest facts. Trump's attacks are not worth a reply.
Oh, we believe in you!
Yes, we believe in you!

The good thing about science is that it's true whether or not you believe in it.

Neil deGrasse Tyson
American astrophysicist

When thinking about how much Trump appeared to despise Dr. Fauci, the English nursery rhyme, "Pop Goes the Weasel" also came to mind.

Trump's Dissing Fauci!

7/19/2020

VERSE:

There's a doctor they say should resign.
He makes me very grouchy.
His approval ratings are better than mine.
I hate Dr. Fauci!

VERSE:

Went to a shrink to help me get by.
And when I laid on the couch, he
Asked me to list all my theories and lies
About Anthony Fauci.

CHORUS:

I say he's too smart and his facts I don't need.
I don't believe what he tells us.
I'll bet he even likes to read.
OK – I am jealous!!

I reached out to the Evangelical community, whose steadfast support of Trump seemed so out of step with the teachings of Jesus. I sent the following poem, a revision of "A Cautionary Tale," to the leaders of the major Evangelical groups in America. Not surprisingly, I received no replies.

Your Lord and Savior is Watching

Please Don't Forsake Him to Follow a False Prophet!
8/4/2020

To my brothers and sisters, please listen
To this message I hope you will heed:
The president you choose to follow
Should be moral in word and in deed.

Take a look at the man in the White House,
Using Bibles as props in his hand,
While protesters are cleared using gasses and fear –
An act for which Christ would not stand!

Does he know that his Savior is listening
To the words from his heart and his mind?
The falsehoods out of his mouth have defiled him. (Matthew 15:11)
Yet supporters appear to be blind.

Children are ripped from their parents
While immigrants' cries are ignored.
What you refuse to do for the least of your brethren
You also deny to your Lord. (Matthew 25:45)

The silence from God-fearing Christians
Speaks louder than anything may.
Just how do you plan to defend it
When you stand there on Judgment Day?

Woe to those who call evil good;
Who put darkness for light in our wake. (Isaiah 5:20)
Return to the teachings that you've understood –
With your vote don't repeat your mistake!

The protests in cities around the country that arose in response to the killing of George Floyd continued for months. The people, who didn't feel valued or heard by the government leaders, kept going. Things got ugly. Outside agitators – some on the left but many, such as The Proud Boys, on the far right – stoked the anger of the protesters and fomented violence. Trump, eager to sow discord, declared that all protesters were anarchists. He then sent unmarked federal agents to take random citizens off the streets without due process. It was frightening to watch. America began to resemble a third-world dictatorship.

This poem is a plea to the protesters in Portland, Oregon, to stop demonstrating and, instead, to come inside to work for real change.

It's Time, Portland!

9/5/2020

You've become Trump's pawn
In his election games.
Your message gone –
You he wrongly blames
For this marathon
Of the rioters' flames.

Time to move inside.
Time to get things done.
Change laws nationwide.
Show you are someone
Trump can't cast aside.
Then this fight you've won.

This poem was written after Trump was said to have called those who served in the military losers and suckers for not having avoided service, as he did. While he denied it vehemently, there's video evidence to the contrary.

Pants on Fire!!

9/8/2020

You have lied every day you've been president.
It comes naturally as breathing to you.
When proof of your lies is so evident,
We can't trust what you say is true.

You've told thousands of lies, verifiable
By video or people who know.
While truth is from sources reliable,
Your falsehoods continue to grow.

We've observed how you call others losers.
This insult is your favorite word.
That's why we believe your accusers.
You cannot deny what we've heard!

When the history books of the future decide
What defined your presidency,
All the times you belittled, bullied, and lied
Will be your lasting legacy.

Once the primary season concluded in August with Joe Biden as the Democratic nominee for president, Trump was eager to begin his savage attacks. "Now I can be vicious!" he declared in a speech at a rally. I thought, "What have you been so far, then?"

I used a word that rhymes with "vicious" at the end of every other line.

A Truly Vicious President

9/15/2020

So, NOW you plan to be vicious
After five years of nothing but hate?
Was your verbal abuse not pernicious
Enough? Your new plan to annihilate
Joe Biden is simply malicious.
Your mocking of him will backfire.
You'll expose with rude comments fictitious –
You're the sucker, the loser, the liar.

Things certainly got vicious. Republican Senator Mitt Romney decided to weigh in on the vitriol, calling politics a "vituperative, hate-filled morass." I learned a new word that day, which inspired this poem, written in limerick style.

Mitt Romney – You're Right!

10/13/2020

Politics today is so crass.
A vituperative, hate-filled morass.
Since 2015
Trump's attempts to demean
Are contagious as COVID, alas!

Now everyone's doing the same,
Using vile words, meant to inflame.
With mudslinging smears
To ignite voters' fears –
Like Trump, they are out to defame.

So, to lower the heat that we face,
Tone it down on both sides in this race,
It must start at the top –
Convince Trump to stop,
For it's he who provokes this disgrace.

A change in tone – in both politics and my poetry writing – was in the air, the night Joe Biden accepted the Democratic nomination for president, when he shared his favorite quote from the Irish poet, Seamus Heaney:

History says
Don't hope on this side of the grave.
But then, once in a lifetime
A longed-for tidal wave
Of justice can rise up,
And hope and history rhyme.

I wrote this poem immediately after his speech:

When Hope and History Rhyme

8/20/2020

Compassion, democracy, character
Are all on the ballot this year.
Restore our country together.
End all the lies and the fear.

Now is the season to head toward the light.
We've seen darkness for too long a time.
Joe Biden will lead toward a future that's bright –
When hope and history rhyme.

The election was hard-fought, resulting in the largest turn-out in history. Over 81 million people voted for Biden and over 74 million voted for Trump. Joe Biden was eventually declared the winner four days after the election, having accrued 273 electoral college votes as of November 7th. With several states still too close to call, Trump refused to concede, declaring himself the winner by insisting that all the mail-in votes in battleground states that were ultimately decided for Biden were fraudulent and should not have been counted. This "Big Lie" persisted through December, and is still believed by many Trump supporters to this day, despite all 50 states' final and official certifications of both their popular ballot counts and electoral college votes on December 14th. On that date, with 306 confirmed electoral votes, Joe Biden was officially declared the president-elect. Trump continued to perpetuate the lie that he won by a landslide, without ever producing any evidence to support his claim.

I decided to try to speak to the Trump supporters with an upbeat parody to the tune of the 1930 song, "Sunny Side of the Street," music by Jimmy McHugh and original lyrics by Dorothy Fields.

On the Biden Side of the Street

12/24/2020

Grab your coat and MAGA hat,
Leave your anger on the doorstep.
Just direct your feet
To the Biden side of the street.

Our new prez is Democrat.
And our spirits now have more pep.
Life will be so sweet
On the Biden side of the street!

I used to wake up with dread
Over something Trump said.
Now the lies that he spread –
They can all go to Mar-a-Lago!

If the truth is good as gold,
I'll be rich as Rockefeller.
No dishonest tweets
On the Biden side of the street!

The challenges to the election results continued into January 2021. Georgia was forced to hand count its ballots and then re-count them a third time. In this, and all of the other contested battleground states, Biden's victories held. Despite recounts having taken place, Trump launched over 60 court cases, challenging the results. Virtually all of his suits, including an appeal to the US Supreme Court, were thrown out, judged either to have no standing or no credible evidence. Still, "The Big Lie" was repeatedly affirmed as truth by Trump, and by his supporters on Fox News and on social media, who insisted, despite a lack of credible proof, that the election was stolen.

Trump believed that he had one final shot at winning – on January 6th, when a joint session of Congress would certify the electoral college votes. Since Mike Pence was to preside over the session, Trump mistakenly assumed that his vice-president had the power to overturn the election results. Upon being informed by Pence that he had no constitutional authority to do so, Trump was furious. He tweeted out an invitation to his supporters to gather in Washington, DC for a rally and protest to "stop the steal," promising, "It will be wild!" Thousands responded to his call, converging on DC on January 6th. They were whipped into a frenzy by President Trump, Donald Trump, Jr., Rudy Giuliani and others. Trump demanded that they march to the Capitol and show great strength in order to reclaim the presidency. Giuliani called for "trial by combat." Don, Jr. threatened anyone who did not support his father by warning, "We are coming for you."

In a matter of minutes the hordes marched down Pennsylvania Avenue, while Trump surreptitiously headed back to the White House. The angry mob violently breached the Capitol, tearing down barricades, smashing windows and breaking doors. They raided offices, urinated on the floors, and smeared feces on the walls. As Trump continued to tweet accusations that his VP lacked the courage to overturn the election, the mob called for Mike Pence to be hanged. The senators, members of congress and vice-president, who had been evacuated from the chamber, hid in utter terror. The police were overrun - some severely beaten. One policeman died and four others later committed suicide. Four insurgents also died during the melee. Meanwhile, Trump watched the riot on TV, "enthralled" at the disruption of the vote certification. He denied Capitol Police requests to summon the National Guard. Mike Pence finally called them, and the uprising was quelled several hours later. Many of the thugs were simply escorted out and allowed to leave. It remains difficult to understand why they were not arrested at the scene.

The insurrection had failed. Congress reconvened several hours later, amid the devastation at the Capitol, and the members carried out their constitutional duty. Joe Biden's victory was certified by the final Electoral College vote tally of 306-232.

The next day, with countless rioters bragging online about what they had done, the arrests began. Those arrested expected that Trump would pardon them. He did not.

The president's words and actions before and during the January 6th insurrection earned him a second impeachment in the House just one week later. Although many Republican senators appeared inclined to support conviction immediately following the riot, the potential threat to their political careers should they do so convinced them to acquit Trump, absolving him of any responsibility for the insurrection.

I have often thought about Trump's legacy. I believe that history will view him harshly, through the lens of his divisive rhetoric and blatant disregard for the truth and the rule of law. The greatest stain on his presidency, however, will likely be the insurrection on Capitol Hill. He is to blame for "The

Big Lie" and the conspiracy theories it spawned, which made it easy for him to incite thousands of people to attack our American democracy in order to keep him in power.

With the election decided, I thought my need to compose long, angry poems and parodies about Trump had vanished. January 6th changed all that. The style of this poem is similar to "Casey at the Bat," recounting the story of that fateful day. I am sure that my dad reached down from heaven to give me the line, "And reveled in the brawl." It sounds just like him!

The Insurrection on Capitol Hill

1/15/2021

It was Wednesday, noon, January 6th
When the crowd heard the president speak:
Let's march to the Capitol side by side!
Show strength — we can't be weak!

I'll be with you as we convince
The congress to overturn
The election Biden stole from us!
(To the White House the coward returned.)

Frenzied and ready to fight, they were,
For the leader they adored,
Based on lies and conspiracies
So that Trump could be restored.

These thugs, who "loved" the thin blue line
Thought the law was on their side,

Savagely beat Capitol police –
Many injured, and one died.

Safe inside the White House,
Trump watched attacks unfold,
The riot he incited
By the base that he controlled.

Did he halt it when the angry mobs
For Pence's death did call?
No, he simply watched with glee –
And reveled in the brawl.

Hours passed. The National Guard
Was sent to clear the mob.
Investigation now reveals
Perhaps an inside job.

Democracy was assaulted,
But the mission unfulfilled.
Trump, now disgraced, impeached again
For the riots on Capitol Hill.

Trump could save the country and
The nation's wounds repair.
Admit that Biden won in an
Election free and fair.

Does he have an ounce of honor left
To speak truth to his base?
His silence just perpetuates
This national disgrace.

Trump's legacy will be the lies
And division he has sown,
But the insurrection on Capitol Hill
Forever he will own.

As Joe Biden was sworn in as the 46th president of the United States on January 20, 2021, I had the same overwhelming feeling of relief that a child has when a school bully has been expelled. Can you imagine Trump and Biden as children in the same class?

The Ballad of Joe Biden, the 46th President

1/20/2021

There once was a school-age bully.
Thought he was the coolest around.
Called the other kids names,
Ruined all of their games
And started fights on the playground.

Soon the popular kids all joined him
So they wouldn't be targeted too.
His approval they sought,
And the meaner they got,
The stronger the bully grew.

He told lies about his classmates,
Took the smaller students' snacks.
The popular crew
Did the same things too.
How would they stop the attacks?

The class was completely divided
Into bullies and victims they use.
One shy kid with a stutter
Began to mutter,
"W-w-we don't have to take this abuse."

We can have a classroom where people are kind.
We can make it uncool to be mean.
If together we stand
And vote in a new plan,
We can fend off the rascals' routine.

With the help of their teacher they persevered.
Each act of aggression was caught.
Bullies' recess was lost,
Now the others are boss,
Having fun while the tough guys do not.

The time for class elections arrived.
To win was the bully's intent.
But the kids knew their mind –
It's more fun to be kind.
That shy leader is now president!

but in the end...
**America chose
the boy who
stuttered**
over the bully

Acknowledgements

In the "nobody does this alone" department, I have many people to thank. My husband, Bill Furman, had no clue when we met that he was getting involved with a rhyming fool, yet, he always stopped to listen to every poem and parody with patience and encouragement – no easy task when I'm so eager to share my latest composition and he's in the middle of a project. I am a very lucky lady.

To my grown children, Brian and Sarah Wolfe, who knew their mom was a little nutty when it came to writing songs and poems but loved me anyway – Thanks for always listening to and liking my creations, even the ones about math! Additional thanks to Sarah's partner, Nate Fulmer, for his support. I am grateful to Brian and his wife, Robyn, for their help, encouragement and participation in the "Vote Mule in 2016" song. The video would not have happened without them.

Thank you to my editors, Ann McGowan, librarian and talented author; Larin Hinson, fellow thespian, teaching colleague, English and theater teacher and poet; and Linda Henley-Smith, childhood friend, teacher, singer, author and humorist. They are all gifted writers and the most amazing human beings. I have learned so much from these extraordinary women!

A special note of appreciation to Lindsey, Andrew, Lucy and the team at Book Production Services/Get It Done LLC. They guided me through the publishing process and made my dream of seeing this book in print a reality!

I am grateful for Raven Audio Books and John Mahoney's expert production of the audio version of my book. It was a great experience!

Barbara Grah and her husband Clinnt Favo, from Grah Photography in Glendale, Arizona, worked their magic creating photos of me for this book. Thank you for putting me at ease and capturing exactly the images I wanted!

A special shout-out to Sadie Rose Casey, web designer extraordinaire, for her skills creating my website, nowigetitproductions.com.

Much appreciation to my friends and family members across the country: Charla McKenna, Coral Frazier, Dana Hall, Gayle Tinker, Glenda Stansell, Judy Bryant, Kim Anderson, Kim Zeitlin Gold, Marianne Roesch, Paul Grad, Sofie De Nardi, and Stuart Sadick. They always knew that a new poem or song would be coming their way soon after any of Trump's debacles. Their comments and support kept me going.

We have friends and family, especially my dear, lifelong friend, Abby Lewis, on the other side of the political aisle who choose to stay in touch, despite our differences. We decided not to allow politics to destroy our relationships. For that I am eternally grateful.

A concluding thank-you to President Joe Biden and Vice-President Kamala Harris, for allowing so many of us to stop feeling verbally abused.

About the Author

Linda is a retired elementary school teacher. Her use of original songs and poems, coupled with the added enticement of edible manipulatives, resulted in her students' favorite math lessons.

Linda enjoys her work as a volunteer, recording books and magazines for the blind. As a seasoned reader and thespian, Linda makes stories and articles spring to life for visually impaired listeners. A life-long baker, she also delights in creating treats (mostly chocolate!) for her family, co-workers and friends.

Linda lives in Arizona with her husband, Bill, and a rapidly growing, young African Sulcata Tortoise named Tortuga.

CPSIA information can be obtained
at www.ICGtesting.com
Printed in the USA
BVHW090352121121
621442BV00010B/361